MW01031352

This book belongs to

_____

First edition 2022
This edition published 2022 by Ascension Publishing Group, LLC

Copyright © 2021 Anno Domini Publishing
www.ad-publishing.co.uk
Text copyright © 2021 Suzy Senior
Illustrations copyright © 2021 Dubravka Kolanovic

Publishing Director: Annette Reynolds
Art Director: Gerald Rogers
Pre-production: GingerPromo, Kev Holt

All rights reserved.

Editorial review for Ascension by Amy Welborn

Scripture passages are from the Revised Standard
Version–Second Catholic Edition © 2006 by the
Division of Christian Education of the National Council of
the Churches of Christ in the United States of America.
Used by permission. All rights reserved.

Ascension
PO Box 1990
West Chester, PA 19380
www.ascensionpress.com
1-800-376-0520

ISBN 978-1-954881-40-2

Printed in the
United States of America
22 23 24 25 26 5 4 3 2 1

A GOOD SAMARITAN STORY

Anyone but Bear

Written by
Suzy Senior

Illustrated by
Dubravka Kolanovic

ASCENSION
Kids

West Chester, PA

Fox was planning a party! He was SO excited. There would be snacks and games and moonlit fun with his neighbors. But, who should he invite? He made a little list.

4

Deer?

Yes, definitely! Everybody loved Deer. She was so beautiful and interesting.

Squirrel?

Of course! He was always very busy digging in the dirt and burying nuts.

But Fox really liked him. Squirrel always brought snacks, too—and the mud was easy enough to wipe off.

What about
Bear? Hmm ... NO!

"ANYONE but Bear!"
Fox muttered.

Bear was fierce-looking
and terrifying, and well ... he
never invited Fox to his parties!

Anyway, Bear lived all the way across the forest. Maybe foxes and bears just aren't meant to be friends, thought Fox.

7

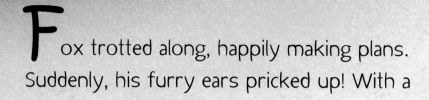

Fox trotted along, happily making plans. Suddenly, his furry ears pricked up! With a

WHOOSH

and a

CLATTER

a shower of rocks tumbled from the mountainside. Fox leaped sideways, but not fast enough!

THUMP!

A rock bounced
off his head.

WHACK!

Another hit
his back leg.

Fox fell to the ground at the side of the path.
His head felt SO heavy. OUCH!

His leg wouldn't seem to move, either. OOOOH!

He cried out, but eventually his head drooped and his eyes closed.

For hours, Fox lay there in the forest as the sun began to sink in the sky.

Then, trip, trap, trip, trap. Fox heard someone coming around the corner.

Wonderful! It was Deer—and Deer always seemed to know just what to do!

But, can you believe it? Deer didn't even stop! She noticed Fox, lying bedraggled and dirty and clearly in pain.

14

"Oh, what a mess!"
Her nose wrinkled.
"I shouldn't really be
seen with anybody in
that state."

Gracefully, Deer turned
away and chose another
path through the forest.

Poor Fox! Still he lay there, injured and sore. He felt a few flakes of snow fall on his ragged fur. Then, scamper, scamper, scamper, scamper, guess what? Squirrel came around the corner!

"Is that Fox?" Squirrel wondered. He came a little closer. "Huh. It really is!" he decided.

But then Squirrel glanced at the pile of nuts he was carrying.

"Hmm," he murmured. "There could be dangerous beasts around! And if I put these nuts down, they might be stolen. Or more rocks might fall, and I might get hurt, too!"

Shaking his fluffy tail, Squirrel scooted off through the forest.

Oh dear! Would ANYONE ever help? Now the snow was falling faster around Fox.

Then thud, thud, thud, thud, someone very LARGE was coming around the corner! Fox's eyes opened very wide!

A big, scratchy paw felt heavy on his leg. And a HUGE, HAIRY, SCARY face loomed right in front of his nose. OH HELP! It could only be... BEAR!

Fox yelped, and tried to struggle!

21

But quickly, Fox's panic began to fade away...
Because, the big face looking down at him
wasn't snarling and scary.

In fact, the face was smiling kindly!
And the huge scratchy paw was carefully
checking Fox's injuries.

22

Before he knew it, those great big Bear paws had scooped him up and were gently carrying Fox home.

23

Back at Fox's den, Bear made Fox comfortable. He even fetched food and water and brought it back for Fox.

24

And then he read a story to the baby fox cubs
and stayed, all through the night, to make sure
Fox was safe and his cubs were sleeping.

When daylight came, Bear waved goodbye and
started out through the snowy forest for home.

But Fox never forgot the love that Bear had shown him.
Anyone could have stopped to help — but Bear actually did!

THE PARABLE OF
THE GOOD SAMARITAN

AND BEHOLD, a lawyer stood up to put him to the test, saying, "Teacher, what shall I do to inherit eternal life?" He said to him, "What is written in the law? What do you read there?" And he answered, "You shall love the Lord your God with all your heart, and with all your soul, and with all your strength, and with all your mind; and your neighbor as yourself." And he said to him, "You have answered right; do this, and you will live."

But he, desiring to justify himself, said to Jesus, "And who is my neighbor?" Jesus replied, "A man was going down from Jerusalem to Jericho, and he fell among robbers, who stripped him and beat him, and departed, leaving him half dead. Now by chance a priest was going down that road; and when he saw him he passed by on the other side. So likewise a Levite, when he came to the place and saw him, passed by on the other side. But a Samaritan, as he journeyed, came to where he was; and when he saw him, he had compassion, and went to him and bound up his wounds, pouring on oil and wine; then he set him on his own beast and brought him to an inn, and took care of him. And the next day he took out two denarii and gave them to the innkeeper, saying, "Take care of him; and whatever more you spend, I will repay you when I come back." Which of these three, do you think, proved neighbor to the man who fell among the robbers?" He said, "The one who showed mercy on him." And Jesus said to him, "Go and do likewise."

–Luke 10:25-37

Who is actually our neighbor? Is it just our friends and the people who live nearby? How are we supposed to love our neighbor? Jesus told us the parable of the Good Samaritan to help us find the answers to these questions.

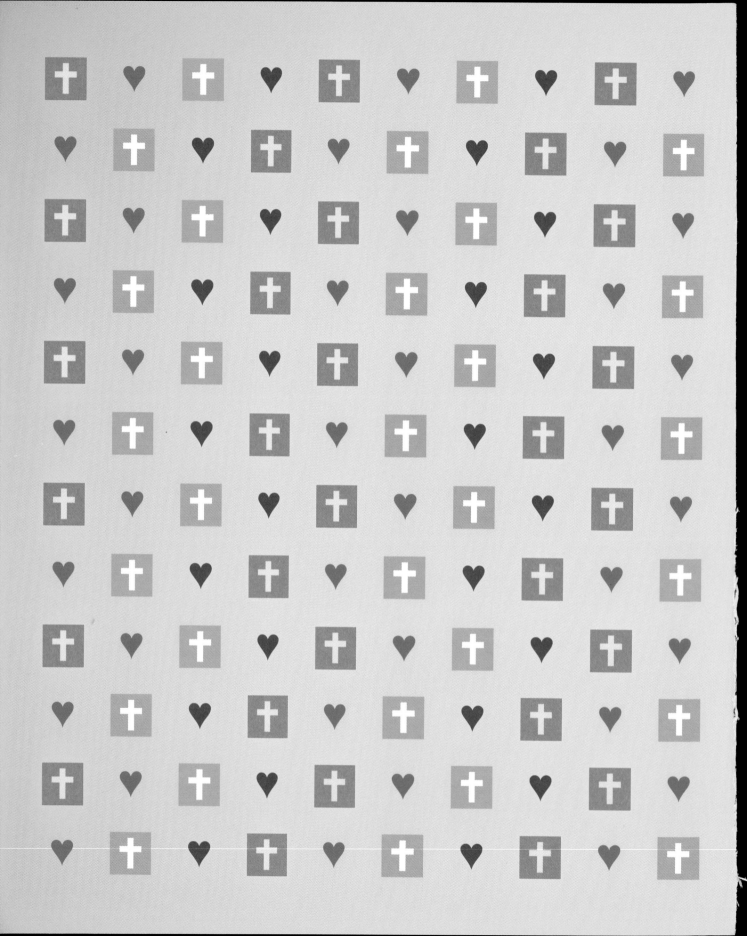